THE COLONY OF
RHODE ISLAND

Greg Roza

PowerKiDS
press™

NEW YORK

Published in 2016 by The Rosen Publishing Group, Inc.
29 East 21st Street, New York, NY 10010

Editor: Sarah Machajewski
Book Design: Andrea Davison-Bartolotta

Photo Credits: Cover, pp. 12–13 (main), 19 SuperStock/Getty Images; p. 4 Wikimedia Commons; p. 5 Nicolaas Visscher II/Wikimedia Commons; pp. 6–7 Universal Images Group/Contributor/Getty Images; pp. 9, 15, 17 North Wind Picture Archives; p. 11 Kean Collection/Archive Photos/Getty Images; p. 13 (inset) Steve Dunwell/Getty Images; p. 16 Time Life Pictures/Mansell/The LIFE Picture Collection/Getty Images; pp. 20–21 (battle), 20 (inset) Library of Congress; p. 21 (inset) Library of Congress/Wikimedia Commons; p. 22 VectorPic/Shutterstock.com.

Library of Congress Cataloging-in-Publication Data

Roza, Greg.
The colony of Rhode Island/ by Greg Roza.
p. cm. — (Spotlight on the 13 colonies: Birth of a nation)
Includes index.
ISBN 978-1-4994-0577-4 (pbk.)
ISBN 978-1-4994-0578-1 (6 pack)
ISBN 978-1-4994-0580-4 (library binding)
1. Rhode Island — History — Colonial period, ca. 1600 - 1775 — Juvenile literature. 2. Rhode Island — History — 1775 - 1865 — Juvenile literature. I. Roza, Greg. II. Title.
F82.R69 2016
974.5'02—d23

Manufactured in the United States of America

CPSIA Compliance Information: Batch #WS15PK: For further information contact Rosen Publishing, New York, New York at 1-800-237-9932.

Contents

Early European Exploration

Rhode Island is bordered by Massachusetts to the north and east and by Connecticut to the west. It's made up of several islands and the land around Narragansett Bay. Although Rhode Island is the smallest state in the United States, its history is far from tiny.

The first recorded European to see the area today called Rhode Island was an Italian explorer working for France. Giovanni da Verrazano sailed into Narragansett Bay in 1524. After discovering a nearby island, Verrazano wrote that it reminded him of the Greek island of Rhodes. This is probably where the state got its name. In 1614, British explorer John Smith mapped the coast of New England, including Rhode Island. Also that year, Dutch sailor Adriaen Block explored land around Long Island Sound.

Explorers found many Native Americans living in Rhode Island, including the Narragansett and the Wampanoag peoples. It wasn't long before Dutch merchants came to Rhode Island to trade with them.

Giovanni da Verrazano

In 1524, Verrazano named the island he discovered Luisa, after the mother of the queen of France. In 1614, Block renamed the island for himself.

Block Island

5N

Moving In

British colonists began to settle along the coast of New England in the 1620s. They founded Plymouth Colony and Massachusetts Bay Colony in present-day Massachusetts. Anglican pastor William Blackstone was the first European to settle in the area that became Boston, on land that soon became part of Massachusetts Bay Colony. Soon after, a group of Puritans arrived and shared the area with him. Blackstone found that the Puritans were **intolerant** of other religions. In 1635, he left Boston to build a farm near a river in present-day Rhode Island, becoming its first European settler.

Roger Williams was another early settler. Williams was forced to leave Massachusetts Bay Colony for questioning its laws. In 1636, Williams and a group of his followers settled along Narragansett Bay. The settlement became the first British town in what later became the colony of Rhode Island. Williams named the settlement Providence, which means "God's guidance," because he felt God had guided him to start this new town.

Roger Williams, right, is shown here meeting with the Narragansett.

Settling In

Blackstone and Williams, Rhode Island's first settlers, were religious **nonconformists** who believed in freedom of religion. Other British settlers who shared their beliefs soon came to Rhode Island. In 1638, John Clarke, William Coddington, and William and Anne Hutchinson founded Portsmouth. Although these settlers had purchased their land from local Native Americans, the Massachusetts colonies wanted to take it over.

In 1644, Roger Williams got a **charter** from Britain's **Parliament**. This protected Providence, Portsmouth, and two other settlements from being taken over by the Massachusetts colonies. The settlements joined under the charter in 1647 and named the colony Rhode Island and Providence **Plantations**.

People who belonged to religions other than that of the established church—such as Quakers, Jews, and French Protestants—weren't welcome in many places in the 1600s. However, Roger Williams welcomed them to settle in Rhode Island. Rhode Island continued to be a location for religious freedom even after it became a state. The Touro Synagogue in Newport opened in 1763. Today, it's the oldest existing Jewish temple in the United States.

Roger Williams traveled to Britain in 1643. In 1644, he returned to Rhode Island with the charter for Providence Plantations. It took until 1647 for the four settlements to reach an agreement under this charter. The settlements were Portsmouth, Newport, Warwick, and Providence.

Unwanted Hostilities

At first, early settlers in Rhode Island had good relationships with Native Americans in the area. Roger Williams had established peaceful relations with the Narragansett Indians. However, settlers in Massachusetts didn't get along with nearby Native Americans, particularly the Wampanoag. The fighting between these groups spilled over into Rhode Island.

In 1675, a Wampanoag chief named Metacomet, known as King Philip to the settlers, led a war against Plymouth Colony. This became known as King Philip's War. The Narragansett Indians had signed a peace treaty with colonists, so they didn't join the fighting. However, they allowed Wampanoag women and children to find safety with them.

Rhode Island didn't join Plymouth Colony in war, but the war affected the colony. In December 1675, a group of Massachusetts colonists burned down a Narragansett village in Rhode Island, killing more than 600 people. The next spring, the Narragansett attacked Providence and other Rhode Island settlements. The war ended in August 1676 after King Philip and many other Native Americans had been killed.

King Philip's War resulted
in the deaths of hundreds
of colonists and thousands
of Native Americans.

Growth and Wealth

The mid-1700s were a time of growth and profit for Rhode Island. Many of the people who settled in the colony had come to make money. The mainland didn't have the best soil for farming, but farmers were able to grow crops such as corn, apples, onions, potatoes, pumpkins, squash, and beans. They also raised cattle. Forests provided lumber for building. Rhode Island's coast was home to fishing and shipbuilding businesses. Coastal towns such as Newport became busy international ports. By the mid-1700s, Providence became the commercial and political center of the colony.

Rhode Island gained more land in the eighteenth century. A 1727 land disagreement with Connecticut was decided in Rhode Island's favor. In 1747, an agreement with Massachusetts also added land to the colony. Adding land to Rhode Island helped the colony grow both in size and wealth. During this time, Rhode Island was led by Samuel Cranston, who served as the colony's governor for 29 years.

Newport Colony House, built 1739

This building is one example of the kind of architecture common in colonial Rhode Island.

Fading Freedom

Rhode Island's 1663 charter gave colonists the freedom to elect their governor and to make their own laws, making it the most independent of the 13 colonies. This situation changed about 100 years later, after the British beat the French in the **French and Indian War**. The British decided to raise the colonists' taxes to help pay for the war and costs to keep British troops in America. In 1764, Parliament passed a tax on molasses, sugar, and other goods. It was called the Sugar Act. The colonists thought it was unfair that a parliament they hadn't elected could tax them in such a way.

Rhode Island presented some of the strongest opposition to Britain of any of the colonies. Rhode Island colonists disobeyed Britain's new laws. They brought molasses into the colony illegally to avoid paying the tax. They attacked British ships and burned them. Later, on May 4, 1776, Rhode Island became the first colony to officially refuse British rule.

This image shows American colonists disapproving of another tax, called the Stamp Act.

15

Rhode Islanders Protest

The Sugar Act was just the first tax on the colonies, and Rhode Island colonists continued to protest Britain's actions. Many Rhode Islanders joined a group called the Sons of Liberty to speak out against the Stamp Act of 1765, which was a tax on anything made of paper. Strong protests throughout the colonies led to the end of this tax that same year. **Smugglers** in Rhode Island didn't openly disobey these unfair taxes. Instead, they sneaked their goods past the tax collectors.

In 1772, the British sent a ship called the *Gaspée* to stop smugglers in Narragansett Bay. On June 9, 1772, the *Gaspée* ran aground near Warwick while it was chasing a smuggler. A group of colonists sailed out to the boat, took it by force, and burned it down. Many historians consider this the colonists' first attack on British forces before the start of the **American Revolution**.

Stamp Act riots

The attack on the *Gaspée* goes down in history as one of Rhode Island's strongest acts against the British.

Declaring Independence

The British grew increasingly angry with each protest that occurred in the colonies. In 1774, Parliament passed four laws called the **Coercive** Acts. These laws—which the colonists called the Intolerable Acts—were meant to punish the colonies for protesting British laws. The relations between Britain and the colonies worsened.

On May 17, 1774, leaders in Providence called for meetings to discuss what to do about British actions. The meetings, which are now called the First Continental Congress, began on September 5, 1774, in Philadelphia, Pennsylvania. Stephen Hopkins and Samuel Ward **represented** Rhode Island.

The American Revolution began on April 19, 1776. Rhode Island announced its independence from Britain on May 4, 1776. It was the first colony to do so. Two months later, the men who gathered during the meetings now known as the Second Continental Congress approved the Declaration of Independence. This **document** was an open letter to King George III of Britain. It declared to the world that the colonies were now **sovereign** states no longer under British rule.

Benjamin Franklin

This painting shows some of the Declaration of Independence's most famous signers, including Benjamin Franklin.

To War!

Before the Sugar Act, Rhode Islanders had the greatest freedom of all colonists, so they were among the first to support the American Revolution. Rhode Island quickly supplied ships, soldiers, and money to help the cause. Rhode Islanders were important leaders in the war. Esek Hopkins of Providence—brother of Stephen Hopkins—was the first commander of the Continental navy. General Nathanael Greene was appointed by George Washington to lead the Continental army in the southern colonies.

Esek Hopkins

British forces occupied Newport in December 1776. In August 1778, General John Sullivan from New Hampshire led troops against the British, but the British held off the attack. This was known as the Battle of Rhode Island. The British left Newport in 1779. The Continental navy could then send ships from this port to attack the British forces in Virginia. In 1781, the Continental army won the Battle of Yorktown in Virginia. This win brought an end to the fighting, and colonists were now citizens of the United States of America.

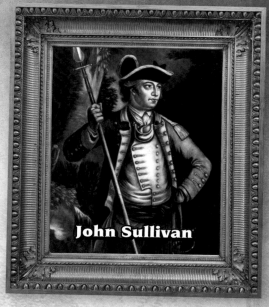

John Sullivan

The Battle of Rhode Island began on August 9, 1778. American troops withdrew in early September, after a 12-day beating by the British.

A Unified Nation

The American Revolution officially ended when Britain and the United States signed the Treaty of Paris in 1783. After the war, the states followed a set of laws called the **Articles of Confederation**. The Articles treated each state more like its own country than as a part of a single country. Serious problems arose, and leaders decided something had to be done.

Rhode Islanders were happy with the Articles of Confederation. They felt a strong central government would be too much like the British government they'd just fought for independence. When a convention was called in 1787 to discuss the Articles of Confederation, Rhode Island didn't send any representatives. The convention approved a new **constitution** in September 1787. Today, these meetings are known as the Constitutional Convention. Rhode Islanders didn't like the new constitution, but the creation of the **Bill of Rights** assured them that their freedoms would be protected. Rhode Island became the thirteenth state to join the United States on May 29, 1790.

Glossary

American Revolution: A war that lasted from 1775 to 1783 in which the American colonists won independence from British rule.

Articles of Confederation: The original constitution of the United States, which was approved in 1781 and replaced by the U.S. Constitution in 1789.

Bill of Rights: The first ten amendments to the U.S. Constitution, which grant rights such as freedom of speech, freedom of worship, and more.

charter: A written statement describing the rights and responsibilities of a government and its citizens.

coercive: Using force to make people do things against their will.

constitution: The set of written laws of a government.

document: A piece of written matter that provides information or that serves as an official record.

French and Indian War: A war between France and Great Britain that took place in North America from 1754 to 1763.

intolerant: Not accepting of views, beliefs, or behaviors that are different from one's own.

nonconformist: A person who has behaviors or views that are different from a majority of people.

parliament: A lawmaking body, or legislature. Also the name of the United Kingdom's legislative branch, which includes the House of Commons and House of Lords.

plantation: In the seventeenth century, another word for a settlement or colony.

represent: To stand for.

smuggler: Someone who moves products into or out of a country illegally.

sovereign: Independent.

Index

Primary Source List

Page 4. *Giovanni Pier Andrea di Bernardo da Verrazzano.* Created by Unknown. Engraving. 1767. Now kept at the New York Public Library, New York, NY.

Page 5. *Belgii Novi. Angliae Novae, et Partis Virginiae Novissima Delinatio.* Created by Nicolaes Visscher. Hand-colored copper engraving. ca. 1651. Now kept at the John Carter Brown Library, Brown University, Providence, RI.

Page 13 (inset). *Newport Colony House.* Designed by Richard Munday and built by Benjamin Wyatt. Brick. Built between 1736 and 1739. The building stands in Newport, Rhode Island.

Page 20 (inset). *Commodore Hopkins, commander in chief of the American Fleet.* Mezzotint on paper published by Thomas Hart. 1776. Now kept at the Library of Congress, Washington, D.C.

Pages 20-21 (main). *The Siege of Rhode Island, taken from Mr. Brindley's House, on the 25th of August, 1778.* Etching and engraving on paper. 1779. Originally published in *The Gentlemen's Magazine.* Now kept at the Library of Congress, Washington, D.C.

Page 21 (inset). *Major General John Sullivan, A distinguish'd officer in the Continental Army.* Mezzotint on paper published by Thomas Hart. 1776. Now kept at the Library of Congress, Washington, D.C.

Websites

Due to the changing nature of Internet links, PowerKids Press has developed an online list of websites related to the subject of this book. This site is updated regularly. Please use this link to access the list: www.powerkidslinks.com/s13c/rhod